Introducing our adult animal coloring book with animal pictures and animal mandalas from pretty easy to really darn hard!

If you can finish coloring all the pictures in this book in under a 100 hours, we'll eat something really yucky!

Thought provoking quotes with every picture. And in case they get you pondering, we included a place to write, draw or doodle next to every page!

It's a nifty coloring book and it's got quotes and it's a journal and also a sketch/doodle pad! Cool right?

We like to think that this book helps us achieve a kind of mental drift. A meditative and thought provoking state of self-discovery where we can drift and wander through whatever is going on inside us while we make something pretty. (Bet you can't say that three times really fast.) Maybe a stray thought will drift on by and we can make a note of what we found going on deep down.

Feel the tension drift down through the pencil (or pen, which can bleed through, but whatever floats your boat, who are we to judge) onto the page, slowly and carefully bringing a world of color to life... "Not now kids, I'm drifting!"

Or you can blaze your hand back and forth across the page like your pen is on fire and your hand is a bucket of water!

It's your book. Whatever makes you *feel* better.

It's all good.

Enjoy.

This book belongs to

Color testing page

Color testing page

"Of all God's creatures, there is only one that cannot be made slave of the lash. That one is the cat. If man could be crossed with the cat it would improve the man, but it would deteriorate the cat."

-Mark Twain

Thoughts, feelings, ideas

A place to doodle

A place to write

A tiger does not need to boast that it is a tiger.
-Nigerian proverb

Thoughts, feelings, ideas

A place to doodle

A place to write

Try to be like a
sea turtle, ...

at ease in
your own shell
-Bill Copeland

Thoughts, feelings, ideas

A place to doodle

A place to write

We are all wolves howling to
the same moon.
-Atticus

Thoughts, feelings, ideas

The lion does not turn around when the small dog barks.
-African proverb

Thoughts, feelings, ideas

A place to doodle

A place to write

When elephants fight,
it is the grass that suffers.
-proverb

Thoughts, feelings, ideas

A place to doodle

A place to write

To use the power of the bison, I had to perform that
part of my vision for the people to see.

Thoughts, feelings, ideas

A place to doodle

A place to write

Butterflies...
are self-propelled flowers.
-RH Heinlein

Thoughts, feelings, ideas

A place to doodle

A place to write

I am fond of pigs. Dogs look up
to us. Cats look down on us. Pigs
treat us as equals.
-Winston Churchill

Thoughts, feelings, ideas

A place to doodle ↘

A place to write ↘

The nature of a panther is that he never attacks. But if anyone attacks or backs it into a corner, the panther comes up to wipe that aggressor or that attacker out.

Thoughts, feelings, ideas

A place to doodle

A place to write

Well as giraffes
say,
you don't get no
leaves unless
you stick your
neck out
-Sid Waddell

Thoughts, feelings, ideas

A place to doodle

A Place to write

A friend is like an eagle, you don't find them flying in flocks.
-Anonymous

Thoughts, feelings, ideas

A place to doodle

A place to write

____
____
____
____
____
____
____
____
____
____
____
____
____

"If you cannot find a good companion
to walk with, walk alone, like an
elephant roaming the jungle. It is
better to be alone than to be with
those who will hinder your progress."
-Buddha

Thoughts, feelings, ideas
A place to doodle
A Place to write

Dogs are not our whole life, but they make our lives whole.
-Roger Caras

Thoughts, feelings, ideas

A place to doodle

A place to write

There is an eagle in me that wants to soar, and there is a hippopotamus in me that wants to wallow in the mud.

- Carl Sandburg

Thoughts, feelings, ideas

A place to doodle

A place to write

It is not only fine feathers that make fine birds.

-Aesop

Thoughts, feelings, ideas

A place to doodle

A place to write

A horse is a thing of beauty... none will tire of looking at him as long as he displays himself in his splendor.

-Xenophon

Thoughts, feelings, ideas

A place to doodle

A place to write

Quick as a hummingbird...she
darts so eagerly, swiftly,
sweetly dipping into the flowers
of my heart.

Thoughts, feelings, ideas

A place to doodle

A place to write

If you chase two rabbits, you catch none.
-Confucius

Thoughts, feelings, ideas

A place to doodle

A place to write

Happiness is a butterfly, which when
pursued, is always just beyond your
grasp, but which, if you will sit down
quietly, may alight upon you.   -
Nathaniel Hawthorne

Thoughts, feelings, ideas

A place to doodle

A place to write

Let the dogs bark,
the lion is still king!
-unknown

Thoughts, feelings, ideas

A place to doodle

A place to write

I am the hawk and there's blood in my feathers, but time is still turning they soon will be dry. And all those who see me and all who believe in me, share in the freedom I feel when I fly.

-John Denver

Thoughts, feelings, ideas

It's surely summer. for there's a swallow: Come one swallow, his
mate will follow, The bird race quicken and wheel and thicken.
-Christina Rossetti

Thoughts, feelings, ideas

A place to doodle

A place to write

Nature's great masterpiece, an elephant; the only harmless great thing.
-John Donne

Thoughts, feelings, ideas

A place to doodle

A place to write

We are part of the earth and it is part of us. The perfumes flowers are our sisters; the deer, the horse, the great eagle: these are our brothers. All things are connected like the blood which unites one's family. - Chief Seattle

Thoughts, feelings, ideas

A place to doodle

A place to write

No human being,
however great,
or powerful,
was ever so free as a fish.
-John Ruskin

Thoughts, feelings, ideas

A place to doodle

A place to write

Then imitate the action of the tiger; stiffen the sinews, summon up the blood.

-William Shakespeare

Thoughts, feelings, ideas

A place to doodle

A place to write

Put another way,
the chimpanzees' closest relative is not the gorilla
but humans.

-Jared Diamon

Thoughts, feelings, ideas

Surely no child, and
few adults, have
ever watched a bird
in flight without envy.
-Isaac Asimov

Thoughts, feelings, ideas

A place to doodle ↷

A place to write ↶

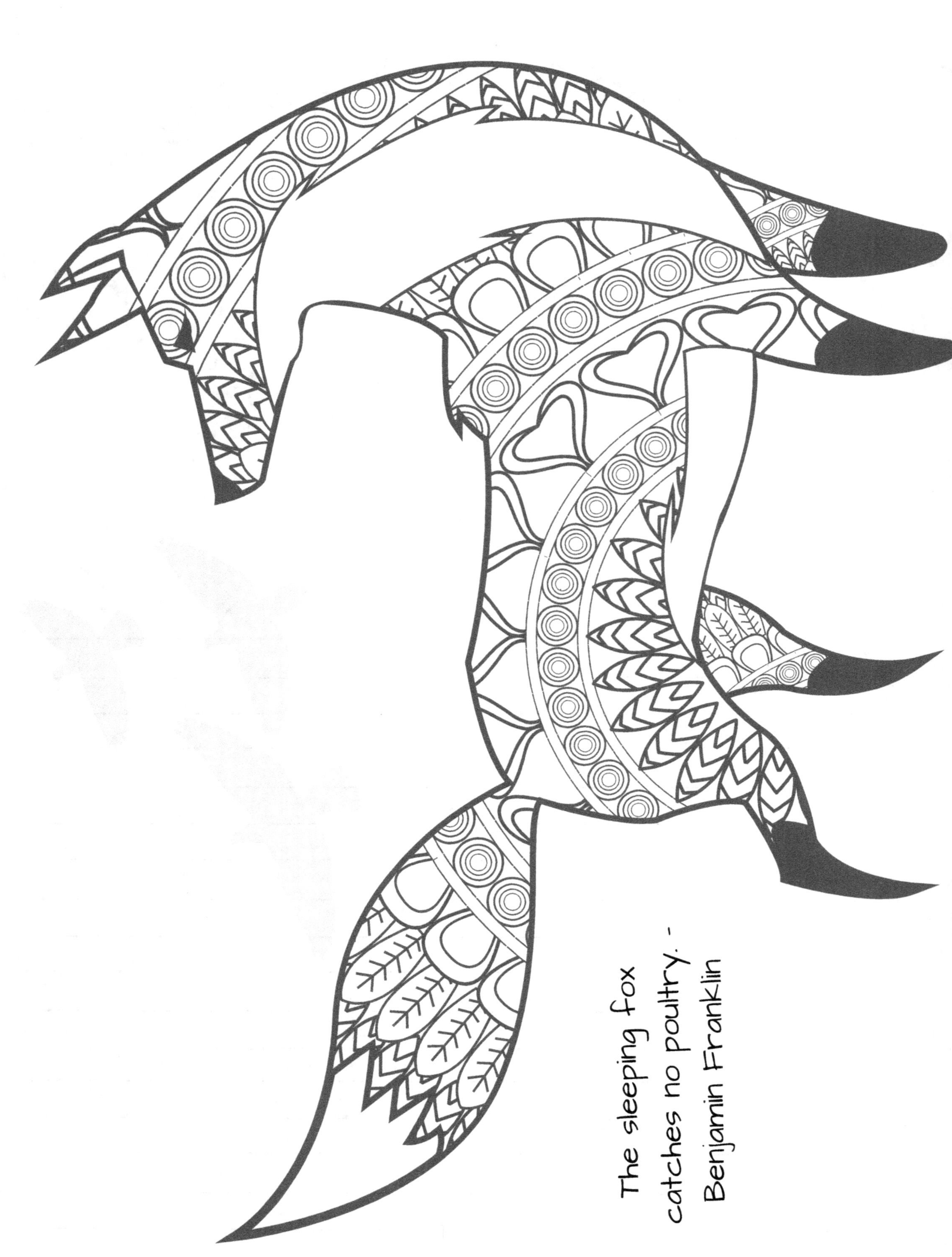

The sleeping fox
catches no poultry. -
Benjamin Franklin

Thoughts, feelings, ideas

A place to doodle

A place to write

I am not afraid of an
army of lions led by a
sheep; I am afraid of
an army of sheep led
by a lion.   -
Alexander the Great

Thoughts, feelings, ideas

A place to doodle

A place to write

May my heart always be open to little birds, who are the secrets of living. Whatever they sing is better than to know. And if men should not hear them - then men are old.

-e. e. cummings

Thoughts, feelings, ideas

A place to doodle

A place to write

God is in the tiger as well as in the lamb.   -John Updike

Thoughts, feelings, ideas

A place to doodle

A place to write

One of the most
striking differences
between a cat and a
lie is that a cat has
only nine lives.
-Mark Twain

Thoughts, feelings, ideas

A place to doodle

A place to write

Just as every drop of the ocean carries the taste of the ocean, so does every moment carry the taste of eternity.

-Sri Nisargadatta Maharaj

Thoughts, feelings, ideas

A place to doodle

A place to write

We must remain as close to the flowers, the grass,and the butterflies as the child is who is not yet so much taller than they are.
-Friedrich Nietzsche

Thoughts, feelings, ideas

A place to doodle

A place to write

Coyote is always out
there waiting, and
coyote is always hungry.
-Navajo Proverb

Thoughts, feelings, ideas
A place to doodle
A place to write

The clamorous owl
that nightly hoots and wonders
At our quaint spirits.   -
William Shakespeare

Thoughts, feelings, ideas

A place to doodle

A place to write

If you pick up a starving dog and make him prosperous he will not bite you. This is the principal difference between a dog and man. - Mark Twain

Thoughts, feelings, ideas
A place to doodle
A place to write

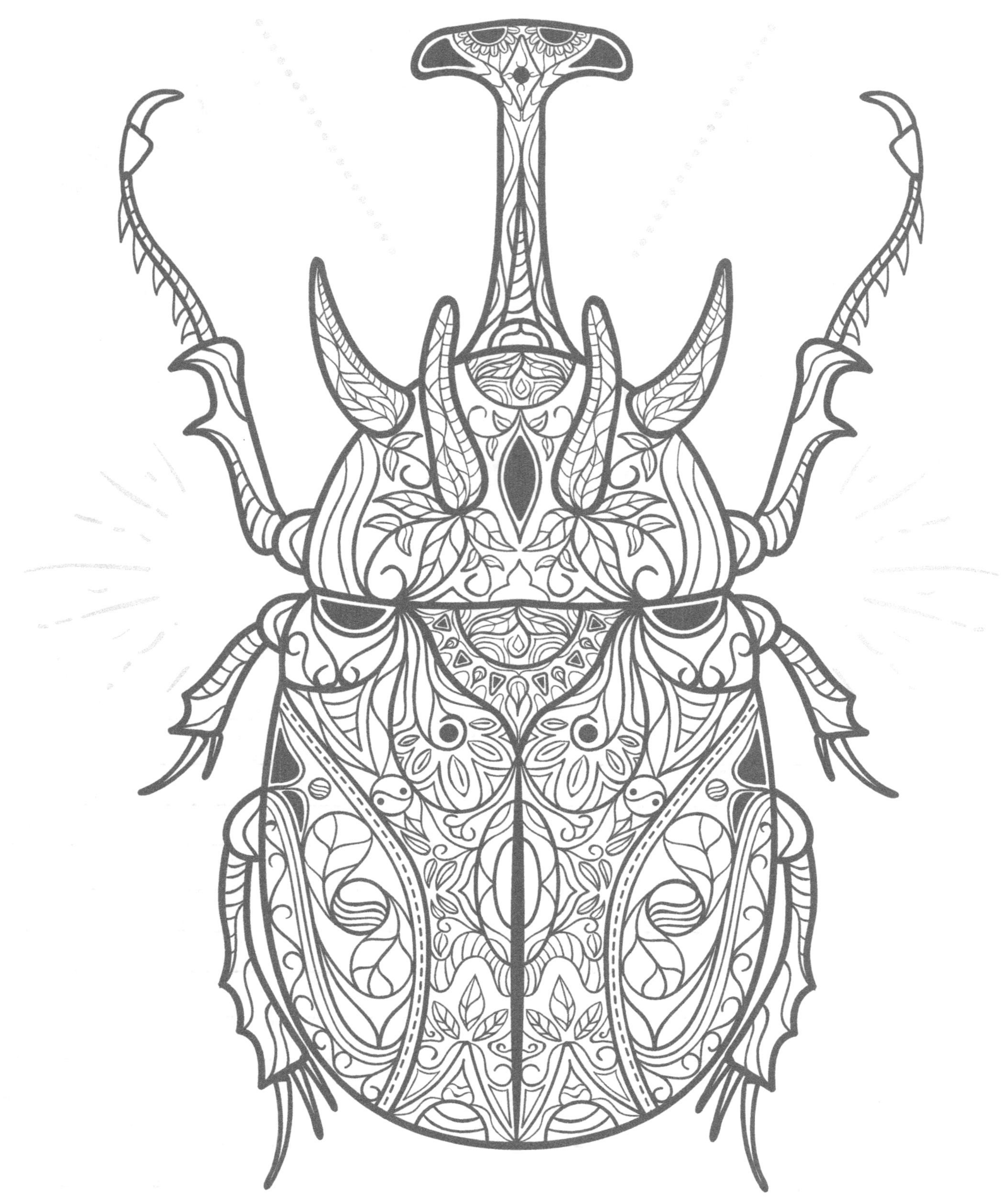

There are 400,000 species of beetles on this planet, but only 10,000 species of mammals....If one could conclude as to the nature of the Creator from a study of creation it would appear that God has an inordinate fondness for stars and beetles.

-John B. S. Haldane

Thoughts, feelings, ideas

The
greatest
achievement
was at first,
and for a time,
a dream.
The oak
sleeps in the
acorn, the bird
waits in the
egg, and in the
highest
vision of the
soul a waking
angel stirs.
Dreams are
the seedlings
of
realities. -
James Allen

Thoughts, feelings, ideas

A place to doodle

A place to write

Look at the sparrows; they do not know what they will do in the next moment. Let us literally live from moment to moment. - Mahatma Gandhi

Thoughts, feelings, ideas

A place to doodle

A place to write

The cat is nature's masterpiece.   -Leonardo da Vinci

Thoughts, feelings, ideas

A place to doodle

A place to write

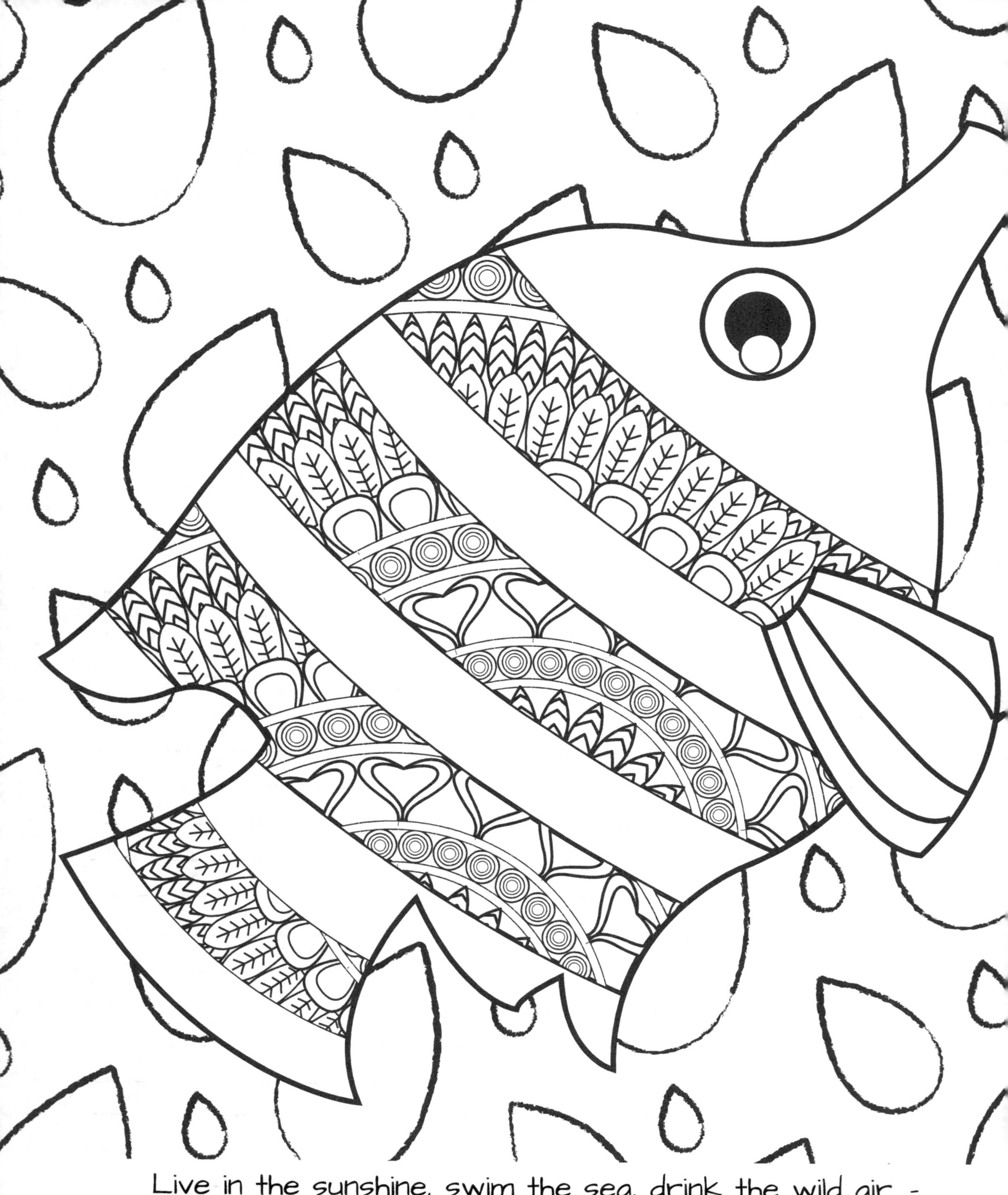

Live in the sunshine, swim the sea, drink the wild air. -
Ralph Waldo Emerson

Thoughts, feelings, ideas

A place to doodle

A place to write

There is no creature among all the Beasts of the world which hath so great and ample demonstration of the power and wisdom of almighty God as the Elephant.
- Edward Topsell

Thoughts, feelings, ideas

A place to doodle

A place to write

A horse never runs so fast as when he has other horses to catch up and outpace.

- Ovid

Thoughts, feelings, ideas

A place to doodle

A place to write

____
____
____
____
____
____
____
____
____
____
____
____
____
____

The Zebra is striped all over so that the Lion can see him and ea[t] him. Some people say he is striped so that the Lion can not see him. These people believe that the stripes of the Zebra simulate the bars of sunlight falling through the tall jungle grasses and that therefore the Zebra is invisible and that the earth is flat.

Will Cuppy

Thoughts, feelings, ideas

A place to doodle

A Place to write

How narrow is the vision that exalts the busyness of
the ant above the singing of the grasshopper.

Thoughts, feelings, ideas
A place to doodle
A place to write

If men had wings and bore black feathers, Few
of them would be clever enough to be crows -
Henry Ward Beecher

Thoughts, feelings, ideas

A place to doodle

A place to write

For me, proof of god is the bear.
-Author

Thoughts, feelings, ideas

A place to doodle

A place to write